Letts **Tour**

The Lake District
The Pennines and Yorkshire Dales

Completely revised by Harry Loftus

Charles Letts & Co Ltd
London, Edinburgh & New York

First published 1969
Completely revised 1974
by Charles Letts and Company Limited
Diary House, Borough Road, London SE1 1DW

Designer: Ben Sands
Cover: Ed Perera
Cover photograph: Masius Wynne-Williams
Photographs: British Tourist Authority (pp 11, 18, 23, 53, 56 and 60);
J. Allan Cash (pp 17 and 34)
Maps: Ray Martin

© Text: Charles Letts and Company Limited
ISBN: 0 850 97141 1

Printed in Great Britain by
McFarlane and Erskine Limited, Dalkeith

How to use your Letts Tour Guide

The best way to see Britain is, for most people, by car. This Tour Guide has been specially designed to lead you—the motorist—to all that is best in its chosen area.

The Lake District, The Pennines and Yorkshire Dales

This series of tours explores three beautiful and much-loved areas: the Lake District, regarded by many as the loveliest and most satisfying part of England; the wild Pennine moorlands, reaching north to the historic Hadrian's Wall; and the Yorkshire Dales, with their sweeping valleys and soaring summits.

Well-known places of interest are visited, and so, too, are many lesser-known spots. The object of this book is to lead you to favoured holiday spas, lakeside resorts, fascinating market towns and delightful villages in the areas, providing you with items of information about the places on your route.

The Tours

There are ten motor tours in this Guide and each of them covers about one hundred miles. If you wish to visit and explore all the places mentioned, you may find that a single tour will provide a very full day of motoring. All the tours are circular, and so you can start and finish a route at any point you may choose. Since there are often children in holiday motoring parties, a list of places likely to appeal to children is given at the end of each tour.

The Maps

The maps (one for each tour and a larger one for the whole area) have been designed specially to show clearly all the information you need—without being unduly technical or too detailed. Readers who usually find map-reading difficult will have no trouble in following the directions and the route. The main approach roads to the tours are also indicated.

Reference Books

The days and the times of opening for houses, castles and museums mentioned in the tours are given; these are correct at the time of going to press. The most recent information can be obtained from the ABC Travel Guide *Historic Houses, Castles and Gardens* which is published annually each January. Details of museums and art galleries are given in *Museums and Art Galleries in Great Britain* published in July each year. The annual AA guide *Britain's Heritage* combines all this information in one book, and is a comprehensive guide to castles, houses, gardens, museums and wild life parks in Britain.

In each tour restaurants with a local reputation for simple meals and good service at an economical price are mentioned. Particulars of other hotels, restaurants and inns are given in the annual reference guide *Hotels and Restaurants in Britain* published by the British Tourist Authority. Two annual selective guides to hotels, restaurants and inns are the *AA Guide to Hotels and Restaurants in Great Britain* and the *AA Budget Guide*. All of these books may be purchased from any bookseller, or consulted at most libraries.

The English Lakes Counties Tourist Board, Ellerthwaite, Windermere, Cumbria; the Northumbria Tourist Board, Prudential Buildings, 140-150 Pilgrim Street, Newcastle-upon-Tyne NE1 6TH; the North West Tourist Board, 119 The Piazza, Piccadilly Plaza, Manchester M1 4AN; and the Yorkshire Tourist Board, 312 Tadcaster Road, York, North Yorkshire YO2 2HF, each publish a wide range of descriptive material about the respective areas covered by these tours. Leaflets and folders can be obtained either direct from the appropriate Tourist Board or from any of the many Tourist Information Centres in the Lake District, the Pennines and the Yorkshire Dales.

Contents

Maps

Tour Maps are on the first or second page of each tour.

From Glasgow

From Edinburgh

A74

A7

Carlisle

A595

M6

Penrith

A66

Keswick
(3)

A592

A595

A6

Windermere
(1)

Kendal
(2)

A590

Lancaster
(9)

A6

M6

Blackpool

Preston

A59

A6

Liverpool

M6

The area covered
by this Tour Guide

Commencing points for tours,
and tour numbers—
Kendal (2)

Tour 1
100 miles

– – – Unclassified roads

1. The Lake District, including Derwentwater and Ullswater

The first three tours in the Guide cover the Lake District, an area of lakes nestling beneath wild crags and made famous by the poetry of Wordsworth, Southey and Coleridge. The routes cross and re-cross at various points, and inevitably overlap because of the scarcity of roads built specifically for motor traffic, but the beauty of this area is such that one can never see the majestic hills or the tranquil lakes too often. This tour, starting from Windermere town, takes in nine of the lakes. It runs through the lovely valleys of Borrowdale and Patterdale, over the stark passes of Honister and Kirkstone, and includes the tranquil towns and villages of Ambleside, Grasmere, Keswick, Penrith and Troutbeck.

Windermere. As seen from Windermere town Lake Windermere could be a disappointment to a first-time visitor. Though the town of slate-roofed houses sprawls 300 feet above the lake, it offers hardly any views of England's largest lake or of the panorama of spectacular hills round about. To get into the spirit of this tour park the car in Windermere, and then walk along the footpath near to the railway station to the top of the 784-ft. Orrest Head. In the 20 minutes or so that this will take, not only will the full 10½-mile length of Lake Windermere be revealed but, also, you will be able to see the vast expanse of Lakeland fells.

Leave Windermere by the A591 in the direction of Troutbeck Bridge, and after one mile you will see on the left signs indicating the Brockhole National Park Centre. On the opposite side of the road is Briery Close.

Brockhole National Park Centre. The first National Park Centre to be opened, the 19th-century house set in 32 acres of garden and woodland contains an exhibition of models, maps and books connected with the local countryside. The centre is open to visitors daily between mid-March and mid-November.

Briery Close is a beautiful, privately-owned woodland with superb displays of daffodils, roses and flowering shrubs at the appropriate times of the year. Briery Close is open to visitors on certain days in summer, and details can be obtained in Windermere.

Beyond the hamlet of Troutbeck Bridge the road skirts the north-east shore of the lake which, at this point, is thickly wooded. The Low Wood Hotel, on the lake shore, offers one of the loveliest views in Lakeland, and the Coniston Old Man and the Langdale Pikes are seen in their splendour from here. Waterhead is reached in 1 mile.

Waterhead is the terminus of the steamer-ferry from Bowness (described in Tour 2, page 19). To the west is Borrans Park, with a bathing place and a fine view down the lake, and next to this is the Borrans Field, with some remains of the small Roman fort of Galava.

Continue along the A591 for ½ mile to Ambleside.

Ambleside is a busy centre for holidaymakers on Lakeland walking tours. The Bridge House, a 17th-century rough-stone structure built originally as a summer house, spans the Stock Beck and is now a National Trust information centre. St. Mary's Church, built by Sir Gilbert Scott in 1854, has a memorial window to William Wordsworth, and a mural depicting the annual rush-bearing festival held in July, when children parade the streets of the town carrying rushes and flowers. One mile to the east is Stockghyll Force, a lovely waterfall set among woods and reached by the lane from the Salutation Hotel. One mile south of Ambleside and just off the A591 is Stagshaw, a woodland garden rich in rhododendrons, azaleas and flowering shrubs and giving fine views across Windermere. It is open daily to the public at all reasonable times.

Continue along the A591 through the Rothay valley, for 1½ miles to Rydal.

Rydal was for much of his life the home of William Wordsworth. Rydal Mount, his former home set in a 4½-acre garden, is now a museum of Wordsworth relics, and is open daily from early March to the end of December. Rydal Mount and the adjacent Dora's Field, noted for the daffodils of which Wordsworth wrote, offer magnificent views of Rydal Water, which inspired the poet so much. The white-walled Nab Cottage, a short distance along the road from Rydal Mount, was occupied for a brief period by Thomas De Quincey.

The A591 hugs the shores of Rydal Water and Grasmere, one of the smallest and most charming of the lakes, before reaching Grasmere village.

Grasmere was the home of Wordsworth and his sister Dorothy from 1799 until 1808. Dove Cottage, where they lived, is open from mid-March to mid-January as a museum, with rooms furnished in the period. In the churchyard, beside the murmuring Rothay, are the graves of the poet, his wife and sister. Thomas De Quincey, who lived for a time at Dove Cottage, is also buried here. On a Thursday every August the village is thronged with visitors for the Grasmere Sports, games which include fell-racing, hound-trailing and Cumberland and Westmorland wrestling and which have been held annually since 1852.

Continuing up the Vale of Rothay the A591 reaches Dunmail Raise (described in Tour 3, page 24) before descending to Wythburn.

Wythburn is a hamlet with a tiny 17th-century church, which is at the southern end of Thirlmere. Enclosed by thick plantations and largely hidden from view, Thirlmere was converted in 1879 into a reservoir to supply water to Manchester, a move still deplored after nearly a century by nature-lovers and conservationists. A dam at the northern end of the reservoir is crossed by an unclassified road leading to the west shore of Thirlmere.

The main road (A591) skirts the steep slopes of Helvellyn (3118 ft.), swings to the west of the Vale of St. John and reaches Keswick.

Keswick is described in Tour 3, page 21. It is a convenient stopping place for refreshments, and the Chaucer House and Red House restaurants are recommended locally.

The route from Keswick is by the B5289 in the direction of Grange-in-Borrowdale, the road skirting the shore of Derwentwater.

Derwentwater is one of the loveliest of the lakes, its surface dotted with small, wooded islands, and its shores a rich mixture of woodland, steep crag and rugged fell. Behind the Lodore Hotel, 3 miles from Keswick, are the famous Lodore Falls, praised by Shelley, but impressive only after a very heavy rainfall.

Continue on B5289 to Grange-in-Borrowdale, a charming village, before entering Borrowdale, and so on to Rosthwaite and Seathwaite.

Borrowdale. Many regard this narrow, densely wooded dale as the most beautiful in Lakeland. Look for the Bowder Stone here, a

Buttermere

gigantic rock which fell from the crags countless centuries ago, and which appears to be delicately balanced on one edge. There is a ladder which can be climbed to the top. Before reaching Rosthwaite you will see, too, the 900-ft. Castle Crag, a steep cone of rock which appears to fill the vale. A 20-minute walk will take you to the top of this rock, and give you a superb view over Derwentwater. The valley changes its character at Seathwaite, which has the unenviable reputation of being one of the wettest places in England, and opens out into a level, green strath. Ahead, and to the left of the B5289, is the 2949-ft. peak of Great Gable, one of the highest and best-known mountains in the area. Despite its formidable appearance, it can be scaled fairly easily if one is properly-equipped and experienced.

B5289 now climbs the Honister Pass, a fierce-looking pass with several 1-in-4 gradients, and the summit at Honister Hause is 1176 ft. above sea-level. The descent to the farm of Gatesgarth is no less steep, after which it is possible to admire the gentle beauty of Buttermere, on the left of the road.

Buttermere village, at the north end of the 1½-mile lake, is a pleasant and welcome resting place, particularly for those tired of riding along the narrow switchback roads. A lane from the church leads south to the Sourmilk Gill waterfalls.

B5289 continues along the east side of Crummock Water, another small and tranquil lake, before reaching Low Lorton.

Lorton Hall (open on Bank Holidays and on other days by appointment) is an attractive 17th-century house in lovely grounds, at which Charles II stayed. Queen Margaret is recorded as staying in the ancient pele tower in 1089.

From Low Lorton follow an unclassified road for High Lorton where the B5292 is joined for the Whinlatter Pass and Braithwaite. A left turn into the A66 at the village brings you along the west shore of Bassenthwaite Lake, the only 'lake' described as such in the Lake District. From the west shore of Bassenthwaite Lake there are fine views of Skiddaw to the right, and after 4½ miles the lake is rounded and a right turn made into the road signposted Castle Inn. Continue for about 1 mile, crossing the River Derwent by the Ouse Bridge, and at the T-junction at the Castle Inn turn right into the A591. The route now goes down the east side of the lake to Keswick (this criss-crossing of roads is unavoidable in the Lake District) joining the A66 for Threlkeld. About 1½ miles before the village, turn right on to an unclassified road signposted 'Stone Circle'. This leads to Castlerigg.

Castlerigg, an early-prehistoric stone circle, stands on a ridge affording fine views of Skiddaw and Saddleback. Threlkeld, which has the kennels of the Blencathra Foxhounds, has a memorial in the churchyard to 45 foxhounds, 'noted veterans of the chase'.

Follow the A66 to Troutbeck Station, then turn right into the A5091, which descends through Matterdale and Dockray to join the A592 on Ullswater (turn right here).

Ullswater is the second largest of the English lakes (7½ miles long) and is usually regarded as the grandest of them. It consists of three distinct reaches, surrounded by the fells and crags of the Helvellyn and Fairfield ranges.

The road (A592) runs under Glencoyne Woods before reaching Glenridding, a small village near the head of the lake, and Patterdale.

Patterdale, the village with the same name as the charming dale, is an attractive centre for those climbing the Helvellyn range. St. Patrick, the patron saint of Ireland, is said to have preached here, and 1 mile north of the town is a roadside holy well which he is believed to have used for baptizing converts.

The road (A592) now climbs to the Kirkstone Pass (1489 ft.) which, until the building of the M6 motorway, was an alternative winter route to Scotland when Shap Fell was snowbound. From the Kirkstone Inn, one of the highest licensed houses in England, descend sharply to reach the Troutbeck Valley. Here turn right on to an unclassified road for Troutbeck.

Troutbeck is a delightful little town with a picturesque inn, The Mortal Man, which is recommended locally for meals. Townend, just off the road, is a fine 17th-century yeoman's house, containing carved woodwork and some excellent furniture; it is open daily, except Mondays and Saturdays, between April and the end of September.

The unclassified road descends to Troutbeck Bridge where the A591 is joined, and a left turn in the direction of Windermere completes the tour.

Appealing to Children

Opportunities for children to stretch their legs and to play are limited on this tour, since the roads are both narrow and busy.

Brockhole National Park Centre, Windermere
Rydal Mount, Wordsworth museum
Dove Cottage, Grasmere
Townend, Troutbeck

Tour 2
65 miles

▪ ▪ Unclassified roads

N

Kendal
A6
A591
A591
A6
A6
Levens Bridge
Sizergh Castle
A590
A590
Lindale
B5277
Grange-over-Sands
Cartmel Priory
Hölker Hall
B5278
B5278
Haverthwaite
A590
B5278
A590
A590
Ulverston
B5281
A5092
A5902
Grizebeck
Broughton-in-Furness
A593
A593
Coniston
B5285
Tarn Hows
B5286
A593
Skelwith Bridge
Clappersgate
B5286
Hawkshead
Sawrey
B5284
Bowness
Ferry
Windermere
Coniston Water

2. The Lake District, including Coniston Water

This tour, like Tour 1 and Tour 3, runs through the Lake District, but it includes also the less-crowded area between Lakeland and Morecambe Bay. As well as following the shores of delightful lakes, the route takes in historic towns like Kendal and Cartmel and great houses such as Sizergh Castle, Levens Hall and Holker Hall.

Kendal known as the 'auld grey town' because of its many fine houses in grey limestone, is the starting point for the tour. Before the opening of the M6 motorway its narrow streets were often jammed with traffic bound to and from Scotland, and until the 1974 changes in local government structure it was the important administrative centre of Westmorland. Now, Kendal has reverted to its old role as a proud and ancient town—Richard Coeur de Lion granted it a barony in 1189—serving a widespread farming community. George Romney, the portrait painter was born here, and lived for many years in a cottage in Redmayne's Yard, just off the main street. Seven of Romney's paintings hang in the town hall. The parish church of Holy Trinity, one of the largest in England, was built in the 13th century, restored in the 19th century, and is notable for its many chapels. In Stricklandgate, a continuation of the main street called Highgate, is the house where Prince Charles Stuart lodged in 1745-46 on journeys to and from Scotland, and on a green hill to the east of the town are the ruins of the Norman castle where Catherine Parr, the sixth and last wife of Henry was born. Much of this history of Kendal is unfolded in the exhibits in the Abbot Hall Museum and Art Gallery, open daily throughout the year, a particularly fine museum in an 18th-century house and the winner of the National Heritage Museum of the Year award in 1973. The Shenstone Restaurant is recommended locally, and there are several smaller cafés in the town.

Leave Kendal by the A6 road signposted 'The South and Lancaster'. After 3½ miles along the Kent valley the gates to Sizergh Castle will be seen on the right.

Sizergh Castle, one of the most impressive castles in this part of the country, was built in 1360 as a stronghold against Scots raiders, and it has been the seat of the Strickland family since that date. The castle contains many fine paintings, ceilings and panelling as well as Jacobite relics, and the Tudor great hall added during restorations which continued to the 18th century is particularly impressive. The house is open on Wednesday afternoons between April to the end of September, and the gardens only on Tuesdays and Thursdays.

Continue along the A6. Immediately after Levens Bridge, the splendid Elizabethan lines of Levens Hall, set in 100 acres of parkland, can be seen on the right.

Levens Hall, the largest Elizabethan mansion in the north-west, contains an impressive collection of paintings and of Charles II furniture. In the grounds is the famous topiary garden laid out by the Frenchman Beaumont in 1689, and, unexpectedly, a unique collection of traction engines and fairground engines. On Sundays in summer these are often set in motion. The house is open on Tuesday, Wednesday, Thursday and Sunday afternoons between May and September, and the gardens daily in this period.

Returning to Levens Bridge, turn left into the A590 for Lindale (6½ miles) and then fork left for Grange-over-Sands.

Grange-over-Sands, a sedate little town sheltered by steep, thickly-wooded slopes and favoured as a place for retirement. Kents Bank, 1 mile south, is the point for which travellers aimed when crossing the treacherous sands of the bay, and the nearby Guides Farm has been the home since the 16th century of the 'oversands guides'. The Commodore and Methven restaurants are recommended locally in Grange.

Leave Grange-over-Sands by a hilly, unclassified road for Cartmel.

Cartmel Priory is sometimes described as the 'cathedral city in miniature'. Founded in 1188 by William Marshall, 1st Earl of Pembroke, the gabled gatehouse near the market cross is, apart from the church, one of the few remains of the priory. The church, however, is rich in superb stained glass and lovely carvings.

From Cartmel follow an unclassified road in the direction of Holker and the B5278, turning right along the road for Holker Hall.

Holker Hall, a delightful 16th- to 19th-century country house with beautiful wood carvings, is set in 22 acres of parkland which contains the biggest herd of fallow deer in Britain. There is a deer enclosure, pets' corner and play area for children, and the house and gardens are open between Easter and mid-October.

Continue along the B5278 to Haverthwaite. Just beyond the village, turn left into the A590. Follow the signposts to Ulverston, a thriving port in the 18th century until the entrance was choked by silt. A590 continues to Barrow-in-Furness and the industrialised Furness peninsula, but our route out of Ulverston is by the B5281 to its junction with the A5092, turning left towards Grizebeck and Broughton-in-Furness.

Broughton-in-Furness is a small and attractive market town overlooking the Duddon estuary, which attracts many visitors because of the walks through woodlands surrounding the town. Broughton Tower, a local landmark, is a 14th-century pele tower re-built in the 18th century.

Coniston Water

The A593 out of Broughton-in-Furness passes through the lovely Duddon valley to Torver, a small village at the south foot of the Coniston Old Man (2635 ft.), and in 3 miles reaches Coniston.

Coniston, half a mile from the head of Coniston Water, once had a copper mining industry, though it is hard to visualise the superb scenery here as ever being a source of industry. However, the disused mines can still be seen to the north of the village. John Ruskin, who is buried at Coniston Church, lived at Brantwood, on the east shore of Coniston Water, until his death in 1900. The Ruskin Museum in Coniston, open daily from March to October, contains many of his MSS, drawings, books and personal relics. The real appeal of Coniston is, however, its situation on the 5½-mile-long Coniston Water, and the magnificent walking and climbing country surrounding it.

Leave Coniston by the A593 through Yewdale. To the right the B5285 will be seen leading to Tarn Hows, one of the prettiest of the lakes. It is worth making the slight detour for the magnificent views of the mountains to be seen from The Tarns. The A593 continues through Yewdale, over the high shoulder of High Arnside to Skelwith Bridge and shortly before the hamlet of Clappersgate passes White Craggs Gardens.

White Craggs Gardens, open daily all the year round, offer a splendid display of shrubs, heathers and, in season, of rhododendrons and azaleas. There are magnificent views from the gardens, and the car park is free.

Beatrix Potter's home, Hill Top

From Clappersgate follow the B5286 through Out Gate to Hawkshead.

Hawkshead, an old village of stone cottages, is certainly one of Lakeland's leading beauty spots. The 15th- to 16th-century church contains the private chapel of the Sandys family, and the nearby Grammar School was founded in 1585 by Edwin Sandys, Archbishop of York. Wordsworth attended the school as a boy, and is thought to have stayed as a lodger at Ann Tyson's cottage in a lane near Red Lion Square in the centre of the village. Wordsworth's name is carved on a desk in the school. The picturesque, old Court House, a relic of a pre-Reformation priory, is now Lakeland's Folk Museum of Rural Crafts, and is open daily, except for Mondays and Thursdays, from Easter to October.

Hawkshead is near the head of Esthwaite Water, and our route, on the B5285, follows the east shore of this 1½-mile-long lake to Near Sawrey, passing Hill Top.

Hill Top, the 17th-century former home of Beatrix Potter, lies just off the road, and is popular with visitors eager to see relics of the famous writer of children's books. The house is open daily from April to October.

The B5285 continues to Far Sawrey and Ferry Nab, where there is a ferry carrying 10 cars at a time across Lake Windermere to Bowness. (There are often long delays in summer, but the alternative is a long detour by road).

Bowness, virtually a suburb of Windermere town, is a popular resort with quaint, narrow streets, and is the headquarters of the Royal Windermere Yacht Club. The 15th-century parish church has some fine 13th-to 15th-century stained glass including some with the stars and stripes arms of the Washington family. If a break for refreshment is needed there are many cafés and restaurants in Windermere, including the Sun, Craigfoot, Elleray, Hide-a-Way, The Knoll and Ravensworth, all of which are recommended locally.

Kendal, the starting point of this tour, is 8 miles from Bowness along the B5284 and a similar distance from Windermere along the busy A591.

Appealing to Children
Abbot Hall Museum, Kendal
Sizergh Castle
Levens Hall with its traction engines
Holker Hall and its deer park
Ruskin Museum, Coniston
Beatrix Potter's home, Hill Top near Sawrey

Tour 3
74 miles

Unclassified roads

3. The Lake District, including the Western Dales

This tour includes the lesser-known western part of the Lake District. It takes in the remote Wastwater and Ennerdale Water, as well as the fine old towns of Keswick, Cockermouth (the birthplace of Wordsworth), the valleys of Great and Little Langdale, the head of the Duddon valley, and the green Eskdale to the west. The Roman fort on the Hardknott Pass and the Viking cross at Gosforth can also be seen; but perhaps the most appealing aspect of this tour is the wonderful and constantly-changing character of the mountains themselves.

Keswick, the starting point for this tour, is an ancient market town sheltered by the steep slopes of Skiddaw (3053 ft.) and about $\frac{1}{2}$ mile from the north end of Derwentwater. In the congested Market Place is the Moot Hall, built in 1813, and along Station Road in the attractive Fitz Park is the Fitz Park Museum, open daily from Good Friday to late October, worth a visit to see the various relics of Hugh Walpole and Robert Southey, and the fine scale model of the Lake District. Near the lower bridge over the Greta are the pencil factories for which Keswick is noted (there is an exhibition hall nearby), and on a hill above is the 18th-century Greta Hall, the home of Robert Southey and of Samuel Taylor Coleridge. Castle Head, a 529-ft. hill south of the town, provides a glorious view of Derwentwater and Bassenthwaite Lake; and Friar's Crag, a headland on Derwentwater, was described by John Ruskin as one of Europe's finest viewpoints. The Chaucer House and Red House restaurants are recommended locally.

Leave Keswick by the A66 in the direction of Threlkeld and Penrith. An unclassified road signposted 'Stone Circle' on the right leads to Castlerigg, an early pre-historic stone circle. Two miles beyond Threlkeld, take the unclassified road to the left signposted 'Mungrisdale'. This road, mainly across open moorland, gives one the chance to stand back, as it were, and to see the majestic panorama of fells and mountains unfolding. On the left, and in the direction of Keswick, is Saddleback (2847 ft.) and behind it Skiddaw (3053 ft.), and so the hills fold and roll in all directions as the road takes us towards Caldbeck. About $3\frac{1}{2}$ miles before Hesket Newmarket, the Horse and Farrier inn will be seen on the right.

Caldbeck is the first village of a reasonable size on this lonely road. Here John Peel, the huntsman of the famous ballad, is buried.

Join the B5299 at the village and go west towards Mealsgate, turning left into the A595 for Cockermouth.

Cockermouth, at the junction of the Cocker with the Derwent, is one of the oldest towns in Cumbria. It was the birthplace in

1770 of William Wordsworth. The house, with the original staircase and fireplaces preserved, is open daily, except Thursday and Sunday afternoons, from April to October. Cockermouth Castle in Castlegate, dating from 1134 and complete with dungeons, was besieged and dismantled during the Civil War, but the great gatehouse and the upper wards survive and are open to the public on Mondays, Wednesdays and Saturdays. South of the town is Moorland Close, a farm house where Fletcher Christian, leader of the Mutiny on the Bounty, was born in 1764. The Appletree restaurant in Main Street is recommended locally.

Take the A5086 out of Cockermouth for Ennerdale Bridge, where a narrow and twisting lane descends rather sharply to Ennerdale Water, a remote lake at the impressive entrance to the wild valley of Ennerdale. This is the only Lakeland valley not accessible by car. From Ennerdale Bridge the A5086 continues to Egremont. Here join the A595 to Gosforth; alternatively, a hilly, unclassified road across moorlands runs into the Calder valley to join the A595 at Calder Bridge. Between Calder Bridge and Gosforth the road passes the huge atomic energy power stations of Calder Hall and Windscale.

Gosforth has a remarkable Viking Cross, probably of the late 10th century, in its churchyard, sculptured with a combination of Norse saga and Christian lore.

An unclassified road from Gosforth signposted 'Wasdale Head' runs towards the secluded hamlet of Nether Wasdale and then along the shore of Wastwater, the deepest and the most sombre of the lakes, with magnificent views of the precipitous Wastwater Screes sweeping down to the opposite shore. This road ends at Wasdale Head.

Wasdale Head is a wild-looking village that is the centre for climbers tackling Sca Fell (3206 ft.), England's highest peak. In the churchyard there are reminders of the hazards presented by these mountains, the graves of rock climbers who have fallen to their death.

Return from Wasdale Head, and at Nether Wasdale fork left for Santon Bridge, a hamlet on the Irt. Turn left here along an unclassified road signposted Eskdale and climb through Miterdale Forest. On the descent to the village of Eskdale Green, a footpath on the right leads to Irton Road Station.

Eskdale is one of the few Lakeland valleys without a lake. The upper reaches are enclosed by an impressive semi-circle of mountains that includes Scafell Pike and Bowfell. About ½ mile beyond Eskdale Green is the King George IV inn, and it may be a welcome refreshment stop before tackling Hard Knott Pass. This pass, with its many hairpin bends and 1 in 3 gradients, is more of an adventure than a meandering drive. Though it only reaches to a height of 1291 ft., its narrowness and its poor surface calls for considerable driving care.

The unclassified road from Eskdale to the pass runs alongside the Ravenglass and Eskdale Railway, a narrow gauge railway built in 1875 to carry iron ore and now restored as a passenger line. The terminal station at Dalegarth is to the left of the road. As the road climbs upwards you will see, unexpectedly, the square fort, with its three double gateways, of Hardknott Castle.

Hardknott Castle was built by the Romans in a highly-strategic position above the pass. This walled and ramparted fort was occupied in the mid-2nd century and is accessible to visitors at any reasonable time.

Eskdale from the top of Hard Knott Pass

From the top of Hard Knott Pass there are splendid views of Eskdale and of the Scafell range of mountains; the road then descends to cross the River Duddon before climbing the narrow and steep Wrynose Pass.

Wrynose Pass links the Bowfell range with the Furness range, and there is a Three Shire Stone by the roadside to mark the meeting points of the old counties of Westmorland, Lancashire and Cumberland.

On the left, and shortly after this point, a steep, narrow lane signposted Elterwater descends to join the B5343 at Elterwater village.

Elterwater, fringed by reeds, is not one of the more attractive lakes, but from its shores one can see the Langdale Pikes.

From Chapel Stile the road ascends Great Langdale and passes the new Dungeon Ghyll Hotel before coming to a halt at the Old Dungeon Ghyll Hotel. Dungeon Ghyll Force, between the hotels, is a waterfall in a narrow ravine with sheer rock walls. Since this is the end of the road, there is no choice but to return back along the B5343, until it joins the A593. Here turn left in the direction of Skelwith Bridge and Ambleside. The route from Ambleside to Keswick by the A591, through Dunmail Raise and Grasmere, is covered in Tour 1, but there are some slight variations to increase one's interest.

Dunmail Raise. Dunmail, the last king of Cumbria whose defeat in 945 brought Cumberland under Scottish rule, gave his name to Dunmail Raise, and a cairn by the roadside was once thought to mark his grave.

Continue along the A591. An unclassified road on the left signposted 'Public Road Round Lake' goes round the west shore of Thirlmere, the reservoir that supplies Manchester with water, before re-joining the A591 south of Keswick. The best views of the lake are from this minor road, and in the north-west corner is the 1520-ft. Raven Crag, a favourite with rock-climbers. Keswick, the starting point of this tour, is less than 6 miles away.

Appealing to Children

Opportunities for children to stretch their legs and to play are limited on this tour, since many of the roads are very narrow and steep and roadside parking can be impracticable, if not impossible.

Fitz Park Museum, Keswick
John Peel's grave, churchyard, Caldbeck
The Castle, Cockermouth
Calder Hall and Windscale atomic energy stations
Ravenglass and Eskdale Railway at Dalegarth station
Hardknott Castle, Hard Knott Pass

4. The Vale of Eden and Weardale

This tour, starting in County Durham, passes through the
Stainmore Gap in the Pennines to the lovely Vale of Eden, which
it descends all the way to Penrith. It then climbs steeply over one
of the most majestic stretches of the Pennine escarpment to
Alston, and runs through Weardale. Blanchland, a fascinating and
unspoiled village, may be taken in on a detour if time allows.
Otherwise, the route passes through the old and quaint towns of
Bowes, Brough, Kirkby Stephen, Appleby and Penrith. Unlike the
steep, twisting roads covered in Tours 1, 2 and 3, the roads on
this route should allow pleasurable driving at moderate speeds,
with opportunities to park the car and picnic in comfort.

Barnard Castle is a delightful old market town with broad streets
and many 18th-century stone houses. Below the octagonal 18th-
century Market House is the 16th-century town mansion,
Blagroves House, and the King's Head Hotel in Market Place was
used much by Charles Dickens while investigating conditions in
Yorkshire schools. The Castle, now largely in ruins, originally
guarded a crossing point across the River Tees, and was re-built in
1112 by Bernard Baliol, an ancestor of the man who founded
Balliol College, Oxford, and confiscated in 1296 following the
revolt of John Baliol, King of Scotland. The history of the district
can be learned best in the Bowes Museum, one of the finest
museums in Britain, and this imposing palace-like building has,
as well, an excellent collection of paintings, porcelain, tapestries
and other examples of European art. The museum is open daily
throughout the year.

Leave Barnard Castle by the A688 to Bowes.

Bowes, a village in an exposed position, was once the Roman fort
of Lavatrae. In an angle of the fort, and built between 1171 and
1187, there is a Norman keep which can be inspected. Driving
through the village, one can see at the west end a large house
which is said to have inspired Charles Dickens to create his
Dotheboys Hall in Nicholas Nickleby.

*Shortly after leaving Bowes, the A688 merges with the A66, and
follows the line of an old Roman road across the Stainmore moors
to Brough. The bleak, lofty Stainmore Gap, which the A66 crosses,
is one of the few breaches in the Pennine range.*

Brough, like so many villages and towns on this route, has a
history steeped in war and bloodshed. The ruined castle, built in
the 11th century, was the home of the 13th Baron Clifford,
nicknamed 'The Butcher' because of his cruelty in the Wars of the
Roses. It stands on the site of the Roman fort Verterae, and is
open to the public throughout the year. Stage coaches used to

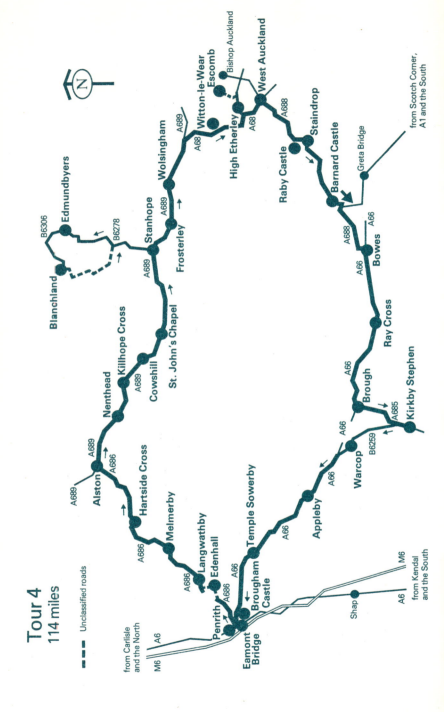

Tour 4
114 miles

- - - Unclassified roads

N

Edmundbyers

B6306

B6278

Blanchland

Stanhope

Wolsingham

A689

Frosterley

A689

Killhope Cross

Cowshill

St. John's Chapel

A689

Nenthead

A689

Hartside Cross

A686

Alston

A689

A686

Melmerby

A686

Langwathby

Edenhall

A686

Penrith

A686

A6

M6

from Carlisle
and the North

Eamont
Bridge

Brougham
Castle

A6

Temple Sowerby

A66

A66

Appleby

A66

Warcop

B6259

A66

Brough

A66

A685

Kirkby Stephen

Ray Cross

A66

Shap

A6

M6

from Kendal
and the South

Bowes

A66

A66

A688

Barnard Castle

Greta Bridge

from Scotch Corner,
A1 and the South

Staindrop

A688

Raby Castle

A68

High Etherley

A68

West Auckland

Witton-le-Wear

Escomb

Bishop Auckland

26

stop here on the long drive from London to Carlisle, with lamps and guards provided on the return journey for the drive across the lonely Stainmore, regarded as the worst coaching road in England.

Leave Brough by the A685 for Kirkby Stephen.

Kirkby Stephen is an attractive town which received its market charter in 1351. A landmark is the 13th-century church of St. Stephen, approached through a large stone portico, and built on the lines of a small cathedral. When Quakers first appeared in the district in the time of Oliver Cromwell, the vicar incited magistrates to take action against them. The town has several fine Georgian houses, and on the outskirts the ruins of Hartley Castle and Pendragon Castle. The Fountain restaurant in Market Street is recommended.

Return north along the A685, then turn left into the B6259 for Warcop, a small village on the River Eden, before re-joining the A66 to Appleby.

Appleby, with a history going back before the Norman Conquest, is dominated by a superb castle, over 800 years old, restored by Lady Anne Clifford, Countess of Pembroke, and now a private residence. Lady Clifford's enthusiasm for building and restoring can be seen on all sides of the town, and the St. Anne's Hospital almshouses (1651), St. Michael's Church and the partly-Norman St. Lawrence Church bear her mark. Two crosses, one at each end of Boroughgate, bear Lady Anne's motto—'Retain your loyalty, preserve your rights'. The Grammar School, which originally stood near St. Lawrence Church in the mid-15th century, had George Washington's brothers, Lawrence and Augustine, as pupils. Appleby Fair in June is famous for its horse-trading and as a meeting place for gipsies. The Bongate, Eden Bridge and Copper Kettle restaurants are all recommended locally.

Continue along the A66 through the Vale of Eden, passing through Temple Sowerby.

Temple Sowerby is an attractive village of red sandstone cottages, with a manor house, Acorn Bank. Once the home of authoress Dorothy Una Ratcliffe, the 16th- to 18th-century house has lovely walled and herb gardens open to inspection on Sundays, Tuesdays, Wednesdays and Thursdays between April and October.

Continue on the A66 in the direction of Penrith, but fork left on to the B6262 for Brougham Castle.

Brougham Castle is yet another castle once restored by Lady Anne Clifford and probably the most interesting castle ruin in northern England. Built between the 12th and 14th centuries, the Keep, the Pagan Tower and a chapel remain in a good state of preservation, and are open daily throughout the year. On the left of the B6262, just after passing under a small footbridge and almost hidden from view, is St. Wilfred's Chapel, built in 1658.

Continue to the Eamont Bridge.

Eamont Bridge the disputed border between England and Scotland before a Papal intervention in 1237. In the village there are two Neolithic earthworks, one known as Arthur's Round Table and the other as Mayburgh, which have puzzled antiquarians for years. The generally-accepted theory is that they were probably burial sites.

From Eamont the A6 runs into Penrith.

Penrith is an attractive market town made more pleasant by the opening of the M6 motorway. Penrith Castle, now no more than a ruin set in a public park, was the home of Ralph Neville, Earl of Westmorland, and was later altered by Richard, Duke of Gloucester, before he became King Richard III. St. Andrew's Church, established in the 13th century, was considerably re-built in the 18th century, and in the graveyard is a group of stones, known as the 'Giant's Grave' and the 'Giant's Thumb', which may have been the burial place of one of the Kings of Cumbria. Penrith has many such interesting, historical features—in Bridge Lane the 'Plague Stone' where, in the 17th century, people washed their money in vinegar as a precaution against the plague; the two 16th-century inns, the Two Lions and the Gloucester Arms, which may have been frequented by Richard of Gloucester. For present-day travellers the Carlton, Glen Cottage and the Waverley restaurants are recommended locally.

Leave Penrith by returning south along the A6 for a short distance before forking left into the A66 and, after one mile, going left again into the A686 for Melmerby and Alston. The road climbs sharply, with many twists and turns, up the long Pennine escarpment with splendid views over the Vale of Eden to the distant Lakeland fells. The descent to Alston over moorlands is equally sharp.

Alston, a picturesque town of stone houses built on either side of a steep, cobbled main street, stands 1000 ft. above sea level and claims to be the highest market town in England—though Buxton in Derbyshire may dispute the claim. For many years the centre of a lead-mining industry, precision steel products are now manufactured in the town. There are some fascinating old houses with outside staircases in the lanes and yards off the main street, including one dated 1681 with a gallery built over the pavement.

Take the A689 out of Alston for Nenthead.

Nenthead, built as a model village during the 19th century for the local lead miners, has an underground canal designed by John Smeaton. It is one of England's highest villages, standing 1415 ft. above sea level.

From Nenthead the road (A689) climbs steeply to Killhope Cross, and before descending to Weardale at Cowshill, reaches the highest point (2056 ft.) of any main road in England. It also gives inspiring

views over moorlands in all directions. From Cowshill, continue to St. John's Chapel and Stanhope.

Stanhope is a quiet holiday centre with good facilities for walkers. There is one rarity in the churchyard, a fossilised tree stump found in a local quarry and believed to be 250 million years old.

This is the point to decide whether to make the 21-mile detour by the B6278 to Blanchland by way of Edmundbyers.

Blanchland, set on the River Derwent, was planned in the early 18th century and can justly claim to be one of Britain's unspoiled villages. Built round the remains of a 12th-century abbey, the village square is entered through the abbey gateway of about 1500. The church and the former abbey storehouse, now the Lord Crewe Arms, overlook the square.

The B6293 continues to Frosterley, a village long noted for its black marble which decorates tombs and pillars in churches and cathedrals throughout the world, and Wolsingham. Four miles beyond Wolsingham, turn right into the A68 for Witton-le-Wear.

Witton-le-Wear is a pleasant village above the north bank of the Wear, with a medieval tower-house re-designed in the 17th century. Witton Castle, across the river, is a 15th-century tower-house considerably re-modelled and extended in the 18th and 19th centuries.

Continue on the A68 to High Etherley and then on to West Auckland. From the A6073, running east from High Etherley to Bishop Auckland, a side road descends to Escomb.

Escomb, a village which has been re-built and restored in recent years, has one of the best-preserved Saxon churches in the country, probably dating back to the 7th century.

From West Auckland follow the A688 in the direction of Staindrop. Before reaching Staindrop, the road passes the boundary of the deer park of Raby Castle, and deer can often be seen from the road.

Raby Castle. The battlemented castle, principally 14th-century, has a fine collection of paintings and is open on Bank Holidays and Wednesdays, Saturdays and Sundays in June, July and September. The gardens, covering about 10 acres, are noted for sweet peas. *Continue to Staindrop.*

Staindrop is a village with an unusually-long village green. The green is believed to have been extended over the years as squatters built cottages, and claimed squatters' rights over the land.

Barnard Castle, the starting point of this tour, is 6 miles from Staindrop along the A688.

Appealing to Children

Bowes Museum, Barnard Castle   Brough Castle
Stanhope churchyard   Deer Park, Raby Castle

Tour 5
100 miles

- - - Unclassified roads

N

Heddon-on-the-Wall
A69 Wylam
A69
B6318
Harlow Hill
Ovingham
B6309
Stagshawbank
Bywell
Halton Chesters
A695
Chollerford
A68
Corbridge
Low Brunton
Dilston
Chesters
Hexham
Carrawburgh
B6318
Langley Castle
Haydon Bridge
A69 A686
A69
Housesteads
Hadrian's Wall
A686
Whitfield
Greenhead
B6318
A686 Alston
B6318
A689
Gilsland
Harper Town
A689
Birdoswald
Kirkhaugh
B6318
Banks
Naworth Castle
A689
Lanercost
Hallbankgate
A69
A6071
Castle Carrock
Brampton
A689
A69
B6413
Kirkoswald

30

5. Hadrian's Wall, the Upper Pennines and Tynedale

This tour follows the course of the great wall of Hadrian, built from Wallsend, near Newcastle upon Tyne, to Bowness-on-Solway on the Solway Firth, and one of the most spectacular relics of Roman Britain. Not only is the Roman Wall of unique historical interest, it traverses some wild and beautiful country, crossing the lovely North Tynedale at Chollerford and reaching the Irthing valley at Gilsland. The tour leaves the Wall near Lanercost Priory, beyond which there is little to see, goes to the handsome town of Brampton before ascending to Alston. The road then crosses the moors and the wooded Allendale to reach the South Tyne, passing through Hexham and Corbridge.

Hadrian's Wall. Before starting this tour it may be useful to know something about the wall, built between AD 120 and 130 protect the northern frontier of Rome's British province. Originally 15-ft. high and topped by 6-ft. battlements, it stretched for 90 miles and was up to 9 feet thick. The wall was patrolled by soldiers, recruited from many parts of the Roman Empire, from so-called 'milecastles', barrack buildings 1620 yards or 1 Roman mile apart. Between the milecastles were two watchtowers at equal distances, serving the dual functions of observation and signalling posts. The troops were quartered in 17 large forts placed at 3- to 7-mile intervals, and these provided granaries, workshops, living quarters and places of worship for anything between 500 and 1000 men. The wall, finally abandoned in AD 383, was built along the crests of hills where possible to take advantage of high ground. A 27-ft.-wide ditch on the northern side of the wall was intended as a further defensive measure, but when Hadrian visited Britain in AD 122 he changed his plan and made cavalry responsible for repelling invaders. For the Roman troops, mostly recruited from countries with a sub-tropical climate, the posting to Hadrian's Wall, swept by fierce winds and rain and often shrouded in mist, must have been one of the least desirable. After the Jacobite rising of 1745, much of the Roman Wall from Wallsend to Sewingshields was broken down and used as a foundation for the Military Road to Carlisle. The first upstanding sections of the eastern side of the wall are at Heddon-on-the-Wall, the starting point of this tour.

Heddon-on-the-Wall is a pleasant village on the north side of the Tyne which is steeped in history. A stone on the river bank dated 1785, and showing the arms of Newcastle, marks the limit for over 600 years of the port of Newcastle. A row of cottages known as Frenchmen's Row, and dated 1786, was occupied by French priests fleeing from the Revolution.

Take the B6318 out of Heddon. On the left will be seen a 100-yard stretch of well-preserved Roman wall, while the road beneath the car's tyres is the Military Road mentioned above, and built from the remains of the eastern section of Hadrian's Wall. Continue along the B6318, passing through Harlow Hill before reaching Halton Chesters and Stagshawbank.

Halton Chesters. Here mounds and ditches remain of the fort of Onnum. Stagshawbank, a further ½ mile along the road, is an open common long famous for the large sheep fair held here, and also the point where the wall was penetrated by the Roman road, Dere Street.

Continue for 3 miles to St. Oswald's

St. Oswald's, a solitary 18th-century chapel in an isolated position north of the Wall, marks the place where St. Oswald, King of Northumbria, pitched his camp before the battle in AD 634, in which he defeated King Cadwalla.

B6318 continues through Low Brunton, where there are good views to the left of the Wall and of a watchtower, to Chollerford and Chesters.

Chesters was a Roman cavalry fort, and in the fine park—it is actually in Chollerford—is the Chesters Museum of items excavated from the fort. The museum is open daily throughout the year. Near the bank of the North Tyne there is also a large and well-preserved bath-house, one of the finest examples in Britain, and when the river is low, two piers of a bridge built by the Romans can be seen.

The B6318 climbs out of the valley to Limestone Corner, where it is possible to see how the ditch alongside the Wall was cut through solid rock. From this point there are splendid views north to the Simonside and Cheviot Hills. The road now runs towards Sewingshields farm and Housesteads, diverging from the Wall. Before reaching Housesteads a halt can be made at the remains of the Temple of Mithras at Carrawburgh which is open daily.

Housesteads, reached by a footpath from the road, is probably the most impressive of the remaining forts, and it is possible to see here the ramparts, gateways, granaries, lavatories and barracks as they were in Roman times. A mile to the west is a fine example of a milecastle, and it is worth following the wall on foot from Housesteads.

The B6318 goes on to the Twice Brewed Inn, and then to Greenhead (6 miles) and Gilsland (2 miles more).

Gilsland, a small spa on the River Irthing, is described in *Guy Mannering* by Sir Walter Scott, who first met his wife here. A section of the Wall has been exposed in the garden of the old vicarage, and on the bank of the Irthing can be seen the abutment of a bridge by which the Wall crossed the river. To the north of Gilsland is the rocket-testing establishment on Spadeadam Waste.

From Gilsland follow an unclassified road on the left to Lanercost.

Lanercost is a small village approached by a beautiful medieval bridge and built round a famous 12th-century priory. Founded by the Augustinian order, the nave was restored in the 18th century and is now used for services, but other parts of the priory are in ruins.

Continue along the unclassified road, passing Naworth Castle, on the left.

Naworth Castle, set in a beautiful park, was built in the 14th century. It passed in 1577 from the Dacre family to 'Belted Will Howard', featured by Scott in *The Lay of the Last Minstrel.*

The minor road soon joins the A69. Here turn right to Brampton, 3 miles away.

Brampton, a handsome town of sandstone buildings on a tributary of the River Irthing, has an octagonal Moot Hall in the cobbled Market Place, and a 19th-century church with richly-coloured windows by William Morris and Burne-Jones. Otherwise, there is little of historical interest; but, on a tour which provides limited opportunities for refreshments, the locally-recommended White Lion inn may prove to be welcome.

Leave Brampton by the A69 in the direction of Haltwhistle, and after a short distance fork right into the A689 for Harper Town, Kirkhaugh and Alston. This road traverses the northern foot of the Pennines, and provides lovely views on all sides. After passing through Kirkhaugh, a straggling hamlet, Whitley Castle, a Roman fort of unknown name, will be seen on the right. From Alston (described in Tour 4, page 28) take the A686 in the direction of Haydon Bridge, a lovely road which crosses the moors before descending to the wooded West Allen valley, finally climbing in zig-zag turns to the moors again before reaching Haydon Bridge. One mile before this small town, Langley Castle is passed on the left.

Langley Castle, a restored 14th-century pele tower, is now used as a banqueting hall, but can be visited at reasonable hours.

From Haydon Bridge follow the A69 to Hexham 7 miles away.

Hexham is a delightful agricultural centre, with a livestock market which handles sheep and cattle from all parts of the north. To the east of the Market Place there is the fine 15th-century Moot Hall or council chamber, and the nearby Manor Office or 14th-century prison is also of interest. The large Priory Church, much of it re-built, still retains the crypt of the original church which was built in AD 678; the Saxon throne in the chancel marks the centre of a medieval circle of sanctuary, providing protection for any fugitives within a radius of 1 mile from the throne or stool. A

Hexham Abbey

34

massive staircase from the south transept once led to the Canons' dormitory. In the town centre is The Sele or Seal, originally a monastic enclosure and now a very fine public park. The Beaumont and the Royal restaurants are recommended locally.

Leave Hexham on the A69 in the direction of Newcastle, passing on the right, Dilston Castle, the ruined 15th-century home of the last Earl of Derwentwater, who was executed for his part in the 1715 Jacobite rising. Corbridge lies a short distance ahead.

Corbridge, an interesting village on the north bank of the Tyne, was once the capital of the Saxon Northumbria, and before that the Roman garrison town of Corstopitum. The excavated buildings of the Roman town, including a huge granary—one of the largest Roman buildings discovered in Britain—lie just to the west of Corbridge and, with the interesting museum of excavated finds, is open daily throughout the year. The church at Corbridge, mostly 13th-century, has a unique Saxon porch-tower with a Roman arch.

Leave Corbridge on the A69 after 1½ miles turn right into an unclassified road for Bywell.

Bywell is an attractive village on the Tyne with two churches, both of them 13th-century, though one of them, St. Andrews', has a Saxon tower. There is also a 15th-century gatehouse in the village.

Continue along the unclassified road to Ovingham, another village with a fine 13th-century church, and on to Wylam, where the birthplace of George Stephenson, of railway fame, can be seen. Take an unclassified road north of Wylam, turning right to rejoin the A69 to Heddon-on-the-Wall, the starting point for the tour.

Appealing to Children

Children are likely to get the most pleasure out of this tour by being allowed to walk along Hadrian's Wall, and to visit some of the Roman forts and milecastles, particularly at Housesteads.

Tour 6
102 miles

Richmond
A6136

A66
A66
Ravensworth
Kirby Hill
A6108
A6108
Reeth
Grinton
B6270
Gunnerside
B6270
Muker
Thwaite
Hardrow
A684
Hawes
Butterubs Pass
Newby Head
B6255
B6255

Middleton-in-Teesdale
Mickleton
Romaldkirk
Cotherstone
A688
Barnard Castle
Greta Bridge
Egglestone Abbey
A688
B6277

High Force
B6277
B6276

Brough
A685
A66
Kirkby Stephen
A685
A683

Sedbergh
A683
Millthrop
Dent
A683

- - - Unclassified roads

N

6. The Pennines, with Teesdale and Swaledale

This tour starts in one of the most attractive towns in North Yorkshire, Richmond, goes northward to the lower part of Teesdale where, if time allows, a detour can be made to the waterfall of High Force. The route then goes across the wild Pennine moorlands to the Vale of Eden, before recrossing the moors to Upper Wensleydale and then over to Swaledale. Towns are rare on this tour, and it will appeal in the main to those who like solitude on a drive. The reward will be a mixture of scenery ranging from the wild grandeur of Swaledale to the open, wooded pastoral peacefulness of Wensleydale.

Richmond, is grandly situated on a steep slope above the Swale. From the top of the 11th-century castle there is one of the finest views in England, a wide panoramic view across the dales to the Vale of York. Dating from the 11th and 12th centuries and one of the earliest to be built in England, Richmond Castle still retains its massive curtain walls and its splendid rectangular keep; it is open daily throughout the year. The Market Place, one of the largest in the country, is the centre of the town's life. There are old houses and shops round it, as well as the lovely Georgian Theatre Royal, one of England's oldest theatres, and the Holy Trinity Church from which the curfew is rung each night at 9 o'clock. The Green Howards Museum, covering the history of the famous regiment, is also in the Market Place.

Leave Richmond by the A6108, turning right into Gallowgate which becomes an unclassified road leading to Kirby Hill and Ravensworth.

Ravensworth is an attractive village built round a large green, near the 14th-century gatehouse and other remains of the once-extensive castle described in Walter Scott's poem 'Rokeby'.

From Ravensworth the minor road continues for 1 mile to the A66. Here turn left to Greta Bridge, 4 miles away.

Greta Bridge is a fine 18th-century bridge by John Carr of York, and near to the entrance of Rokeby Hall associated with Sir Walter Scott. A lane north of the park leads to the meeting of the rivers Tees and Greta, a scene painted by Turner and Cotman. Near by stands the 15th-century Mortham Tower in a lovely setting above the Greta. Charles Dickens stayed in the fine, old 'Morritt Arms' inn, formerly named the 'George'.

A short distance beyond the park, turn right into an unclassified road signposted Egglestone Abbey and Barnard Castle.

Egglestone Abbey, set on a knoll above the Tees, was built mostly in the late-12th and 13th centuries, and the ruins can be visited daily throughout the year.

Continue past the abbey to the junction with the B6277, and then turn right to follow the signs for Barnard Castle.

Barnard Castle is described in Tour 4, page 25.

Take the B6277 northwards out of Barnard Castle for Cotherstone and Romaldkirk.

Romaldkirk is a delightful village set round a large, irregular green which is overlooked by grey stone almshouses. Lanes lead from the village to reservoirs on the moors above, and the outlook from high up is very impressive.

The B6277 continues to Mickleton, Middleton-in-Teesdale, and, a further 4½ miles up the Tees valley, High Force.

Middleton-in-Teesdale is a quarrying town, where a 16th-century detached bell tower can be seen near a modern church. High Force is a magnificent waterfall, the foaming water gushing over a 70-ft.-high basalt cliff to tumble into the beautiful, wooded glen below.

Return along the B6277 and beyond Middleton-in-Teesdale turn right into the B6276 to climb the desolate Lunesdale for 7 miles before descending to join the A66 a short distance east of Brough. This lonely, minor moorland road runs alongside the river Lune for part of the way, and on the left can be seen the reservoirs above Romaldkirk.

Brough is described in Tour 4, page 25.

Continue south along the A685 in the direction of Kirkby Stephen.

Kirkby Stephen (also described in Tour 4, page 27) may be a convenient stopping place for refreshments. The Fountain restaurant in Market Street is recommended locally.

Leave Kirkby Stephen on the A683 for Millthrop and Sedbergh, a stone-built market town famous for its public school. Near the church there is an unclassified road signposted 'Dentdale', and this leads by way of the village of Dent to the dale, one of the smallest and most delightful of the Yorkshire dales.

Dent, with its cobbled main street and colourful houses, is a charming, little town which used to be the centre of the knitted woollen stocking industry. The large church has 13th-century nave arcades, but is otherwise of the 16th century, and there is some good Jacobean woodwork to be found in it. The fountain in the centre of the town is a monument to a noted geologist, Adam Sedgwick, who was born in Dent.

The unclassified road climbs sharply through the upper reaches of Dentdale, with the prominent Whernside (2419 ft.) seen to the right and ahead, and reaches the B6255 where a left turn will lead down the remote Widdale to Hawes.

Hawes, is described in Tour 10, page 61).

*Follow the A684 out of Hawes in the direction of Leyburn, but after
a short distance turn left into an unclassified road which crosses the
river Ure, turning left again and then right to climb steeply to the
Buttertubs Pass. Before the climb is made, however, the road to
Hardrow, a hamlet near the Hardrow Force, may be followed.
After heavy rain the Force is an impressive waterfall.*

The Buttertubs Pass, rising 1726 ft. on the watershed between
Wensleydale and Swaledale, takes its names from the Buttertubs,
a series of deep fissures in the limestone. These are not the largest
of the Pennine potholes, but they are the closest to a motor road.
On the north side of the pass, it is worthwhile pulling into the side
of the road to view the wild scenery that can be seen in every
direction, including Great Shunner Fell to the west.

*The unclassified road continues to Thwaite, a pleasant hamlet at the
foot of Kisdon hill. Here a 2-mile detour can be made by turning left
into the B6270 to Keld, a lovely greystone village hemmed in by the
fells, with several impressive waterfalls within easy walking distance.
Returning to Thwaite by the B6270, the route continues to Muker,
once the centre of the Swaledale lead-mining industry, and on to
Reeth and Grinton. This stretch of the route reveals that Swaledale
is the narrowest, deepest and, possibly, the most remote of the
Yorkshire dales.*

Grinton was a thriving little village in the 19th century, when the
moors above were alive with mining activities, but it is mainly
noteworthy now for its attractive three-arched bridge and for its
unusually large church. First built by the Normans but mainly in
the Perpendicular style, it was in medieval times the burial place
for the dead from the whole of Swaledale. A mile before the
village, a narrow road on the left leads to prehistoric earthworks,
probably dating back to the Iron Age, and from this spot there are
superb views of Swaledale.

*The B6270 continues towards Richmond for 4½ miles before joining
the A6108, and passes the remains of Marrick Priory, a former
12th-century house for Benedictine nuns, now incorporated into the
parish church of Marrick.*

Appealing to Children

This tour takes in spectacular scenery which will be of interest to
adults, but not necessarily to children. However, there is no
shortage of places where children can be safely allowed to stretch
their legs and to run wild. Three places of interest in Richmond
and in Barnard Castle will captivate most children.

The Castle, Richmond
Green Howards Museum, Richmond
Bowes Museum, Barnard Castle

From Richmond and the North
A6108
Leyburn
From Hawes   A684   **Wensley**
West Burton   **West Witton**   **Middleham**
B6160   **East Witton**   **Jervaulx Abbey**
A6108
Kidstones Pass   A6108
A6108
Masham
Buckden
Kettlewell   **Kirkby Malzeard**
B6160   **Winksley**
Kilnsey   **Fountains Abbey**
Grassington   A61
Threshfield   **Linton**   **Wormald Green**
Burnsall   **Ripley**
A61
Bolton Abbey   A59   Knaresborough
A59   B6160
Skipton   **Harrogate**
From Liverpool   A6034   **Addingham**   **Pannal**   A1
A65   A61
Silsden   **Burley-in-Wharfedale**
Steeton   **Ilkley**   A660   A659   A659
A629   A6038   **Otley**   **Pool**   **Harewood**
Keighley   Guiseley
A65
From Manchester   From Bradford   From Leeds   From the South

N

Unclassified roads

Tour 7
94 miles

40

7. The Yorkshire Dales: Wharfedale and Wensleydale

This tour takes in two of the best-loved dales, the long, deep Wharfedale and the broad, pastoral Wensleydale, both with their many delightful villages. It includes, also, the resorts of Ilkley and Harrogate, the interesting monastic remains of Bolton Abbey, Jervaulx Abbey and Fountains Abbey, the impressive ruins of Middleham Castle, and the model villages of Harewood and Ripley, which also has a castle.

Ilkley, the starting point of the tour, is probably best known for its association with the song 'On Ilkla Moor baht 'at' and, to strangers, this could result in a mistaken impression of a pleasant town. Situated on the south bank of the river Wharfe, with a gracious 17th-century bridge spanning the river, Ilkley is popular both as a holiday resort and as a spa. The Manor House Museum (open daily except Mondays) is situated in a Tudor house built on the site of the Roman fort of Olicana, and its exhibits provide a good insight into the town's long history. All Saints' Church is 16th-century with three Saxon crosses in the churchyard. Southwest of the town, above the head of Hebers Ghyll, is the 'Swastika Stone', a carved relic of the Bronze or Iron Age. The moorland road on the south-east passes the Cow and Calf Rocks, a favourite practice slope for rock climbers. The Crescent restaurant in Ilkley is recommended locally.

Leave Ilkley by the A65 road in the direction of Skipton, and on the outskirts of Addingham turn right into the B6160 for Bolton Bridge and on to Bolton Abbey.

Bolton Abbey, with its priory, founded in 1151, is so charmingly situated on the river Wharfe as to have attracted the attention of many artists, including Landseer. The priory ruins, open daily, are set among meadows and woods, and the nave, which has been extensively repaired and lengthened, is the parish church. The attraction of the village lies in its setting and in the many pleasant walks around it. Two miles along the A59 in the direction of Harrogate is Beamsley Hospital, a curious circular almhouse dated 1593.

Continue for 2 miles along the B6160, the road following the Wharfe, to reach the ruins of Barden Tower.

Barden Tower, a massive tower-house built in the 15th century, was restored in 1659 by Lady Anne Clifford, then living at Skipton Castle. The ruins, open daily throughout the year, are more impressive because of their beautiful setting. A 17th-century chapel attached to a cottage in the courtyard is worth inspection.

Continue to Burnsall.

Burnsall. Every mile of the road through Wharfedale opens up new vistas, and Burnsall is situated picturesquely on a lovely reach of the river. The church is 16th-century with a late-Saxon or Norman font, and the fine old Grammar School was founded in 1602. To the east is Appletreewick (approached by an unclassified road on the right of the B6160), an attractive hamlet with Parcevall Hall, an Elizabethan house in beautiful gardens, near by. The gardens of Parcevall Hall are open on Tuesday and Wednesday afternoons from May to September.

The dale road (B6160) continues to Linton.

Linton is a delightful village of grey houses grouped round a green, where the river, now no more than a stream, is crossed by three bridges—a pack-horse bridge, a clapper bridge and a modern bridge for traffic. The imposing building in the village is Fountaine's Hospital, founded in 1721 as an almshouse for six poor women, but now housing men as well.

The B6160 continues up the narrowing valley to Kilnsey, a hamlet under the precipitous buttress of Kilnsey Crag popular with anglers, and to Kettlewell (which is described in Tour 8, page 48). Continue to Buckden and the Kidstones Pass.

Buckden, is the highest village in Wharfedale, and the inn provides the last opportunity for refreshment, before the road climbs sharply through Cray to the summit of the Kidstones Pass. The Kidstones Pass is on the watershed between Wharfedale and Wensleydale, and commands superb views over the Pennine moorlands.

The descent through Bishopdale to West Burton is steady, and soon afterwards the B6160 joins the A684 to Wensley.

Wensley, which gives its name to the dale, is a quiet, grey stone village which was once a thriving commercial centre. First granted a royal charter in 1202, the town went into decline in 1563 following an outbreak of the plague. The 13th- to 14th-century church beside the river, with its Restoration font and 15th-century screen, is an indication of Wensley's earlier importance.

Continue along the A684 from Wensley, and fork right into the A6108 to Middleham.

Middleham is well-known for its racing stables and attractive in its own right because of its situation on a hill above the river Ure. There are several interesting Georgian houses set round the market-place, but the most impressive building is the 12th-century Middleham Castle, now largely in ruins, which was once a stronghold of the Earl of Warwick and a favourite retreat of Richard III. The massive keep, said to be one of the largest in England, is enclosed by a 13th-century wall, and is open as an Ancient Monument on weekdays and Sunday afternoons throughout the year. Beyond the castle is the moor, where horses from the dozen or so local racing stables can be seen in training.

The A6108 crosses Ulshaw Bridge, a lovely bridge dating from 1674, before reaching East Witton and, 1½ miles beyond the village, Jervaulx Abbey.

Jervaulx Abbey, once a great Cistercian abbey, founded in the 12th century and later dissolved by Henry VIII, has a quiet charm about its ruins if it is less impressive than the remains of Fountains Abbey. Little remains of the church, but the surviving parts of the domestic buildings, in particular the dormitories and the chapter house, are in good preservation, and enable us to form an impression of what day-to-day life in this great monastic house was like. Jervaulx Abbey is open to view throughout the year.

Continue on A6108 to Masham.

Masham is the centre of the Wensleydale cheese industry, much of this pleasant cheese now coming from small factories instead of from farmhouse kitchens. The church, mainly of the 15th century, has a partly-Norman steeple, and in the churchyard is a fragmented Saxon cross.

From Masham follow an unclassified road through Grewelthorpe and Kirkby Malzeard, another cheese-making village with a splendid partly-13th-century church, and on through Winksley and, after crossing the B6265, on to Fountains Abbey (9½ miles from Masham).

Fountains Abbey, once the wealthiest Cistercian house in England, is certainly now one of the loveliest left behind. Dating from 1132 (the nave and transepts) to 1526 (the tower), the ruins have a majestic splendour which is quite unmatched. The Chapel of the Nine Altars is a masterpiece of rare delicacy, the Refectory can only be described as impressive and the Cellarium, 300 feet long, is breath-taking. The most remarkable feature of all, perhaps, is the wonderful state of preservation of the abbey through the centuries. The abbey is open daily throughout the year, and the adjacent Fountains Hall, a Jacobean mansion with period furniture and tapestries, is open daily from late March to late October. A footpath from the abbey leads for nearly one mile through the impressive grounds of Studley Park, laid out in the 18th century as a formal landscape garden. Ripon (described in Tour 8, page 46) is 3 miles to the east, and the Old Deanery restaurant is recommended locally.

Leave Fountains Abbey by an unclassified road signposted Markington, and after 3½ miles turn left for Wormald Green before joining the A61. Here turn right for Ripley and Harrogate (both described in Tour 8). From Harrogate continue on the A61, through Pannal to the junction with the A659 where the A61 takes a left bend towards Harewood.

Harewood (pronounced Harwood) is a model village built by John Carr in the late 18th century outside the park of Harewood House. Harewood House, home of the Earls of Harewood, was also designed by Carr, and this splendid mansion with its state rooms, pictures, Chippendale furniture and redecorated Doric Hall and gallery is particularly worth visiting. The park, laid out by 'Capability' Brown, has a bird garden containing 200 species, as well as a cafeteria and children's playground. The 15th-century Harewood parish church is in the park, and it contains a monument to Chief Justice Gascoigne, said by Shakespeare to have committed to prison the Prince of Wales (later Henry V) for contempt of court. Harewood House is open to the public daily from Easter to mid October. North of the house are the ruins of Harewood Castle, a 14th-century tower-house.

Return on the A61 in the direction of Harrogate, but turn left into the A659 for Pool and Otley.

Otley is an old market and manufacturing town with a fine 15th-century church with a good Georgian pulpit. In the churchyard is the grim 'Railway Tunnel' memorial to the men who lost their lives building Bramhope railway tunnel between 1845 and 1849. Thomas Chippendale, the noted cabinet-maker, was born in Otley, and a plaque in the Market Place marks the site of his birthplace in 1718.

Follow the A660 out of Otley for Burley-in-Wharfedale, then fork right into the A65 to return to Ilkley.

Appealing to Children
The Manor House Museum, Ilkley
Barden Tower, near Bolton Abbey
The three bridges at Linton
Middleham Castle, Middleham
Fountains Abbey
Harewood House and park

8. The Yorkshire Dales: Swaledale and Nidderdale

This tour, notable for its many interesting churches and picturesque villages, runs at first through the rich pastoral country of the Vale of York, and takes in the old town of Knaresborough, the Roman remains at Aldborough, the fine Georgian mansion of Newby Hall, and the delightful cathedral city of Ripon. It ascends Swaledale, one of the most beautiful of the Yorkshire Dales, crosses the Pennine moorlands, and turns south to cross the moors again for the lower part of Nidderdale.

Harrogate is a popular spa town which, in recent years, has become well-known as a centre for conferences. The Royal Baths, built in 1897, contain a variety of medicinal-treatment baths and include, also, a large winter garden. The Royal Pump Room (open daily during the summer and week-ends only in the winter) contains the old sulphur well which originally brought the town its fame, and there is, too, a small museum of local history and Victoriana. The town, which has a dignified Victorian charm, is noted for its floral displays, and the Valley Gardens are particularly fine. About one mile west of the town centre, along the Otley Road, are the Harlow Car Gardens, a 60-acre trial ground for experimental gardening, open daily throughout the year and of considerable interest to horticulturalists.

Leave Harrogate by the A61 to The Stray, turning left into York Place and then joining the A59 to Knaresborough.

Knaresborough, situated on a cliff high above the river Nidd, is a sedate town of Georgian houses in narrow streets that will repay closer attention. The remains of the 14th-century Knaresborough Castle, where Richard II was imprisoned in 1399, are impressively sited on a cliff overlooking the Nidd, and are open daily from Easter to late October. On the opposite bank of the river, and reached by the High Bridge, there is the damp and rather eerie Dropping Well, where an assortment of everyday objects are being petrified by the lime in the water dropping from the rock face. Near by is Mother Shipton's Cave, reputedly the birthplace of a legendary prophetess, who predicted: 'World then to an end shall come, in Nineteen hundred and eighty one'. On a more practical note the Conyngham Hall zoo (open daily from Easter to the end of October) has a large collection of wild animals and a tropical marine aquarium.

Leave Knaresborough by the A6055 (B6166) towards Minskip, then turn right into an unclassified road to Aldborough.

Aldborough has extensive remains of the Roman town of Isurium, the most northerly town to be built by the Romans. Portions of the boundary wall can be seen near the church, there are two

Tour 8
84 miles

- - - Unclassified roads

Aldborough
Minskip
Bridge Hewick
Skelton
Boroughbridge
Knaresborough
A6055
Spofforth
A59
A661
Pannal
A658
From Bradford
Harrogate
A61
A61
A61
Ripley
B6165
A61
Summer Bridge
B6165
Pateley Bridge
B6265
Greenhow Hill
A59
Blubberhouses
From Manchester
Bolton Bridge
Grassington
B6265
B6160
Kettlewell
B6160
Buckden
B6160
Aysgarth
A684
B6160
Castle Bolton
Wensley
A684
Leyburn
A684
Constable Burton
Patrick Brompton
A684
A684
B6268
Bedale
A684
Snape
Well
West Tanfield
A6108
A6108
Ripon
B6265
West Tanfield

tessellated pavements at the village inn and a small museum (open daily throughout the year) has a collection of objects unearthed from the site.

Continue along an unclassified road to Boroughbridge.

Boroughbridge, now by-passed by the busy A1, was once an important staging point for the stage coaches plying between London and Edinburgh, and there are some old inns remaining where the horses were stabled. In the market place is a well, 250 ft. deep, with a modern canopy. West of the A1 are the Devil's Arrows, three monoliths from 16 ft. to 22 ft. high and probably dating back to the Bronze Age. Why they are here is a puzzle, since prehistoric men are believed to have dragged the huge pieces of millstone grit at least 10 miles to their present site. The Blinking Owl restaurant is recommended locally.

Go north along the B6265 for a short distance before turning left into an unclassified road for Skelton, near which are the gates of Newby Hall.

Newby Hall is a fine Queen Anne house with two wings built by Robert Adam. There is a good collection of statues in a specially-built gallery, as well as some splendid Gobelin tapestries and excellent Chippendale furniture. The grounds covering 25 acres contain a miniature railway and a river on which there are cruises. Both Hall and grounds are open on Wednesdays, Thursdays, Saturdays and Sundays between Easter and the middle of October.

Follow an unclassified road on to Bridge Hewick before turning left on to the B6265 for Ripon.

Ripon is an old market town with narrow, winding streets over which the cathedral looms. Built from the 12th century onwards on the site of an Anglo-Saxon church, the cathedral contains much lovely wood-carving, notably on the bishop's throne and the choir stalls. The focal point of the town is the market square where there is a 90 ft.-high cross, and from here every night at 9 o'clock the town's official horn-blower, the Wakeman or watchkeeper, sounds the curfew. The Wakeman's Museum (open daily throughout the year) is in a house dating back to the 13th century, and contains objects of local and historical interest. There are interesting remains of two ancient hospitals, St. Anne and St. Mary Magdalen in the town, and east of the station the remains of the Sharrow Cross. The Old Deanery restaurant is recommended locally.

Leave Ripon by the A61 going north, but after a ½ mile fork left into the A6108 for West Tanfield.

West Tanfield is an attractive village on a bank of the river Ure. The 15th-century church has fine wood-carvings by Robert Thompson, the Yorkshire craftsman, and the tombs of the

Marmions, who lived at the nearby castle, of which the picturesque 15th-century gatehouse remains.

Leave West Tanfield by an unclassified road for Snape and Snape Castle.

Snape Castle was once the home of Catherine Parr, 6th wife of Henry VIII. The ruins of the 15th- to 16th-century castle, a stronghold of the Neville and Cecil families, are not open to the public, but the delightful late 15th-century chapel is accessible during daylight hours.

Take an unclassified road from Snape through Mile House to the junction with the B6268; here turn right for Bedale.

Bedale is a picturesque market town with a wide main street which has held a market for nearly 800 years. Old brick and whitewash houses lining this street provide a pleasing picture. The mainly 13th- and 14th-century church, with its lofty tower arch and vaulted crypt, is one of the finest in North Yorkshire, and facing it is the 18th-century Bedale Hall. The hall now contains a small museum of ancient crafts, and is open on Tuesdays from May to September.

Leave Bedale on the A684, passing through Patrick Brompton, which has a 12th- to 14th-century church with an outstanding chancel and nave arcades, and Constable Burton, and then on to Leyburn.

Leyburn, a busy country town, stands above the river Ure and is regarded as the gateway to Wensleydale. The 'Shawl', a 2-mile-long limestone scar reached by a footpath from the town, gives an entrancing view of the dale.

Continue along the A684 to Wensley, where an unclassified road to the right leads to Bolton Castle.

Bolton Castle is a partly-restored stronghold dating back to the late 14th century. Mary, Queen of Scots, was imprisoned here in 1568-69; later the castle was besieged and eventually taken in 1645. Open daily, except Monday, throughout the year, the castle has an interesting Dales Museum including a replica of an early Dales kitchen.

Follow the unclassified road west until it joins with the A684, then turn in the direction of Aysgarth.

Aysgarth is a Wensleydale village with some notable waterfalls in the vicinity. The most noteworthy of these is the Aysgarth Force, reached by a footpath to the north of the church, and in an old corn mill by the falls is an interesting carriage museum (open daily from Easter to late October). The mill, which went out of use for grinding corn as recently as 1968, now houses 60 vehicles, including rare horse-drawn carriages, sleighs and the last woollen dray to be used in Bradford.

Going east of Aysgarth along the A684, turn right after a short distance into the B6160. This narrow, moorland road climbs sharply to Buckden (described in Tour 7, page 42), the highest village in Wharfedale proper, and on the left is the landmark of Buckden Pike.

Kettlewell, one of the prettiest villages of upper Wharfedale, shelters below the 2310-ft. Great Whernside and has a lovely old stone bridge crossing the river Wharfe. This is a favourite centre for rock-climbers, and it is common to see experienced climbers on Kilnsey Crag on fine week-ends. Kettlewell has several inns and cafes, and makes a good halting-place for refreshments.

Take the unclassified road on the east bank of the river, below a series of limestone scars, to Conistone and Grassington.

Grassington is the principal village of upper Wharfedale. It is beautifully situated, with a medieval bridge spanning the Wharfe, and a cobbled market place that is the meeting point for several narrow streets.

Take the B6265 towards Hebden, then over the open Hebden and Appletreewick moors to the Stump Cross Caverns.

Stump Cross Caverns (open daily in summer; week-ends only in winter) are a series of caves and passages beneath the Craven limestone with interesting stalactite formations.

The B6265 continues to Greenhow Hill before descending steeply to Pateley Bridge.

Pateley Bridge is an old-fashioned market town at the entrance to the narrow and beautiful upper part of Nidderdale. Just off the B6265, near Foster Beck, is the Watermill Inn, a former flax mill dating back to the mid-17th century. The wheel, 36 ft. in diameter and weighing about 30 tons, was built in 1800, and is the second largest in existence in Britain.

One mile outside Pateley Bridge join the B6165 for Summer Bridge. To the north of this little village are Brimham Rocks, an outcrop of millstone grit moulded into weird and fascinating shapes by the weather. The B6165 continues to Ripley.

Ripley is a model village with a rare example of a 'Weeping Cross' in the churchyard and with village stocks. Ripley Castle (open on Sundays from Easter to September) has been the home of the Ingilby family since 1350, and is set in fine gardens and grounds.

From Ripley the A61 returns to Harrogate.

Appealing to Children

The Castle   Conyngham Hall Zoo, Knaresborough
The Devil's Arrows, Boroughbridge   Newby Hall grounds
Bolton Castle   Aysgarth Falls Carriage Museum
Stump Cross Caverns   Watermill Inn, Pateley Bridge

Tour 9
112 miles

- - - Unclassified roads

N

From Harrogate and the Great North Road

From Leeds and the Great North Road

Addingham

A59

Bolton Bridge

A65

A629

A65

Keighley

Steeton

A629

From Manchester

A6033

Haworth

Laneshaw Bridge

Skipton

Kildwick

Gargrave

Colne

A6068

Blacko

Hellifield

Barrowford

A682

A65

Long Preston

Settle

Downham

A671

Giggleswick

A65

A59

Clapham

Chatburn

A59

Clitheroe

Ingleton

Browsholme Hall

Great Mitton

B6246

Whalley

Cowan Bridge

Dunsop Bridge

Whitewell

A683

Kirkby Lonsdale

A65

Hornby

Trough of Bowland

A683

Tunstall

Caton

A683

Melling

Halton

A6

A65

From Kendal and the North

M6

A6

Lancaster

A6

M6

From Liverpool and the South

50

9. The Lower Pennines: Ribblesdale to Lunesdale

This tour embraces a wide variety of contrasting scenery: the gentle upper Airedale, the green Lunesdale or Lonsdale, the lonely moors of the Forest of Bowland and the wilder Pennine moors. It starts in Lancaster, a Roman town with great historical associations, takes in the caves and waterfalls near Ingleton, the village of Haworth, famous for its association with the Bronte sisters, and includes the abbey remains at Whalley.

Lancaster is a much-neglected town which motor traffic now by-passes, and through which trains to Scotland travel at high speed. Taking its name from the Roman *castrum* or camp which was sited beside the river Lune at this point, the town has a fine medieval castle, a magnificent priory and several Georgian houses of character. Lancaster Castle (open generally on week-days except when the Crown court is sitting) dominates the town from its position on a hill above the river, and has a Norman keep with many later additions. John of Gaunt, Duke of Lancaster and father of Henry IV was responsible for many of the enlargements, and Elizabeth I added fortifications as a defence against the Armada. The magnificent priory and parish church of St. Mary, which stands alongside the castle, is mainly of the 15th century, though parts date back to Saxon times, and the wood-carvings on the 14th-century choir stalls are among the finest in England. The Old Town Hall in Market Street, a Georgian building, is now the interesting Lancaster Museum (open daily) with local exhibits as well as being the regimental museum of the King's Own Royal Lancashire Regiment. Walk along the tree-lined quay on the Lune, past the Custom House with its graceful Ionic columns, and it is hard to imagine that in the 18th century Lancaster was a port handling a bigger tonnage than Liverpool.

Leave the town by the A6 north, crossing the Lune by Skerton Bridge, and shortly afterwards taking an unclassified road on the right for Halton.

Halton is a peaceful village with a church with a 15th-century tower. In the churchyard stands an 11th-century cross carved with scenes from the Norse saga of Sigurd the Volsung. A mile beyond the village, and near where the road crosses the river, is the Crook o'Lune, a beautiful, wooded ravine that has been painted many times by artists, most notably by Turner. To the north-east is Aughton, a picturesque, hillside village where the thriller writer E. C. Lorac lived during the years before his death in 1958.

After crossing the Lune the road joins the A683, and then continues through the green Lunesdale to Hornby and Melling.

Hornby, on the river Wenning, has the remains of a 16th-century castle whose keep can be seen for miles around. The keep was built by Sir Edward Stanley, who later became Lord Monteagle, after the Battle of Flodden Field in 1513. His coat of arms decorates the unusual octagonal tower of Hornby church, and was put there as a thanksgiving for his safe return from the battlefield. Melling has several charming 18th-century houses, and a 15th-century church containing a set of musical instruments once used to accompany the choir. Tunstall, 2 miles beyond Melling, is the 'Brocklebridge' of *Jane Eyre*.

Continue to Kirkby Lonsdale.

Kirkby Lonsdale, set on a hill above the Lune, is a lovely town much favoured by coach parties of holidaymakers from Morecambe. Among the town's fine buildings are the partly 14th- to 15th-century church, the 17th-century Manor House and the 18th-century Fountain House. The town is the 'Lowton' of *Jane Eyre*. South of Kirkby Lonsdale is the picturesque 13th-century Devil's Bridge spanning the Lune, and beneath it a pool where salmon can often be seen leaping. The Red Dragon Inn is recommended locally.

Cross the Lune again by the A65, and continue in the direction of Settle by way of Cowan Bridge.

Cowan Bridge is a hamlet on the Leck Beck, and on the right of the road are the old buildings of the Clergy Daughters' School, a school that appears to have had unhappy memories for Charlotte Bronte. The school, now the Casterton Girls' School, has been sited for some years at Casterton, north-east of Kirkby Lonsdale.

Beyond Cowan Bridge continue on the A65 to Ingleton.

Ingleton stands at the junction of two becks, the Greta and the Kingsdale, and is a noted centre of the Craven country of caves and waterfalls. Among the most notable and the most accessible are the Skirwith Cave and the White Scar Caves (both open daily during the summer) which are near the B6255 road to Hawes. These are on the lower slopes of Ingleborough (2373 ft.), probably the major landmark of the Pennine hills. From the village there are walks which follow the waterfalls through a series of ravines, and the most impressive after heavy rain are the Thornton Force and the Beezley Falls.

An unclassified road from Ingleton runs south for a ½ mile before joining the A65 to Clapham.

Clapham, a delightful village of grey stone houses in bright gardens, lies in a wooded valley shut in by limestone hills. Ingleborough Cave, reached in 1¼ miles by a footpath, has a series of passages and chambers extending for one-third of a mile, and festooned with beautifully-coloured stalactites and stalagmites in a variety of shapes. A mile further along this path is Gaping Gill,

Waterfall at Ingleton Glen

a fearsome pothole down which a jet of water hurtles from a height of over 300 feet. This cave is only to be explored in the company of experts.

Continue to Giggleswick. Beside the Clapham road, 1 mile before Giggleswick is reached, is an unusual ebbing and flowing well.

Giggleswick, on the west bank of the Ribble, is an old-fashioned village with 17th- to 18th-century houses and a fine church in the Perpendicular style. The carved pulpit is dated 1680, and there is an ancient reading desk. Giggleswick School, with a prominent domed chapel, is a public school founded in 1512.

Continue to Settle.

Settle, situated at a point where the Ribble flows through the Aire Gap, is a delightful town which combines the dual roles of being a major market centre and a focal point for walkers and pot-holers. It has several attractive 17th- and 18th-century houses, and at Townhead, to the north of the church, there is a remarkable private museum of bones of Stone Age and Iron Age man, as well as of elephants and rhinoceroses, found within the district. The museum owner, Mr. Tot Lord, will usually show his collection on application.

Leave Settle by the A65 which runs down Ribblesdale to Long Preston and Hellifield, and then enters Airedale for Gargrave and Skipton.

Skipton (described in Tour 10, page 59) is a pleasant town in which to seek refreshment, and the Midland restaurant is recommended locally.

Leave Skipton by the A629 Keighley road which passes through the Aire valley to Kildwick.

Kildwick, where the Aire is crossed by a bridge that is partly medieval, has a 14th- to 17th-century church which is known as the 'Lang Kirk of Craven'. It has an unusually ornate font cover, and in the churchyard there is a 19th-century tomb carved in the shape of an organ.

Continue to Keighley.

Keighley, which stands at the confluence of the rivers Aire and Worth, is a manufacturing town which has carefully preserved its history and character. Cliffe Castle, a 19th-century mansion with formal gardens and a well-wooded park, has been converted to a museum (open daily) with a good collection of local 'bygones', craft workshops and musical instruments. There is a free car park to the rear of the castle. Two miles out of the town, on the Bradford road, is the 17th-century East Riddlesden Hall with the curious wheel windows typical of some West Riding manors. The Hall (open daily from March to October) contains a collection of furniture, pictures and armour, and there is an old tithe barn.

*Leave Keighley by the A629 up the Worth Valley, and in 2 miles
fork right for Haworth which is reached in 1 mile.*

Haworth, a grey, old-fashioned village with a steep main street,
has become a place of pilgrimage to lovers of the Bronte novels.
The famous parsonage, to which the Rev. Patrick Bronte brought
his family in 1820, is at the top of the main street. It is now the
Bronte Parsonage Museum (open weekdays and Sunday
afternoons), with relics of Charlotte and Emily Bronte. Their
graves are in the churchyard below the old parsonage. The Black
Bull Inn, a popular calling place for visitors, is where Branwell
Bronte drank himself to death, and on the moors are the ruins of
High Withins, the setting for *Wuthering Heights.* The revived
Worth Valley Railway, which runs the 5 miles from Keighley to
Oxenhope, has its headquarters at Haworth station. It is
maintained as a museum and rolling-stock depot (open Saturdays
and Sundays and certain weekdays in summer), and includes the
largest collection of veteran steam and diesel locomotives in
private ownership.

*Follow an unclassified road from Haworth church over the wild
moorlands of the Forest of Trawden to Laneshaw Bridge, then turn
left into the A6068 for Colne.*

Colne, on a ridge above the valley of the Colne Water, is a
manufacturing town. In Sun Street there is an unusual museum
(open Wednesdays, Fridays, Saturdays and Sunday afternoons),
the British In India Museum, with dioramas, a working model
railway, coins, medals and stamps illustrating British government
in India up to 1947. The restored 16th-century church has a rare
example of mobile stocks in its churchyard.

*Take the A56 out of Colne, then fork right into the B6247 for
Barrowford. Here the A682 is joined, but at Blacko take a minor
road on the left to Downham.*

Downham, at the foot of Pendle Hill, is a delightful village of
stone-built houses which claims, not without some justification,
to be the prettiest village in Lancashire. The Hall, parts of it
dating back to the 13th century, was the home for generations
of the powerful Assheton family, and it has associations with the
Civil War. The 15th-century church has a font given by John
Paslew, the last abbot of Whalley.

*Continue along the unclassified road to Chatburn, then turn left
into the A59 for Clitheroe.*

Clitheroe, a pleasant market town that conceals its antiquity, was
granted its charter in the 12th century. A ruined Norman keep on
a limestone cliff at the end of the main street is all that remains of
Clitheroe Castle (open Tuesdays, Thursdays and Saturdays, May to
September), but this was one of the greatest strongholds of the
Royalists in the Civil War. From the wall round the castle there

is a good view of Pendle Hill (1831 ft.) associated with the Lancashire witches. From the summit of the hill it is possible, on a clear day, to see York Minister to the east and the Irish Sea to the west.

Continue along the A59, east of the Ribble, to Whalley 4 miles away.

Whalley, a village on the Calder, is notable for the remains of a 13th-century Cistercian abbey, founded by monks from Cheshire. The remains include part of the chapter house and a splendid 14th-century gateway. The abbey ruins are open daily throughout the year, but the 15th-century Abbot's lodgings, now used as a church conference centre, are not normally accessible to casual visitors. The parish church of St. Mary is mainly 13th-century with some 15th-century additions. There is a wealth of fine, carved woodwork in the church, the choir stalls being outstanding. The churchyard is of unusual interest, containing three Saxon crosses and several gravestones dating back to the 13th century. Two more-recent gravestones are remarkable for recording dates that never existed—April 31, 1752, and February 30, 1819.

Leave Whalley by the B6246 across the Ribble to Great Mitton.

Great Mitton has an interesting church, mainly of about 1300, with a 15th-century tower, 15th- 16th-century woodwork, and family monuments of the Shireburns, who lived at Stoneyhurst, an Elizabethan mansion now a part of the well-known Roman Catholic Stoneyhurst College.

John of Gaunt's Gate, Lancaster Castle

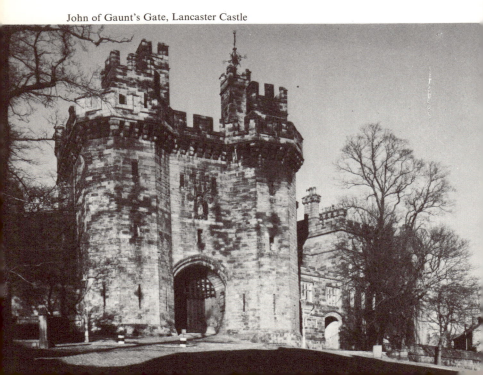

Turn right into the B6243, then take an unclassified road to Browsholme Hall.

Browsholme Hall is a fine Tudor house, altered in the 17th and 18th centuries, with Elizabethan and Stuart panelling, pictures and furniture. It has been the home of the Bowland Forest Rangers for at least 600 years, and contains interesting relics from the forest. It is open Tuesday afternoons, Thursdays, Saturdays and Sundays from Easter to mid October.

From Browsholme Hall follow the unclassified road to Whitewell, a village beautifully situated on the Hodder, then up the valley of the Hodder to Dunsop Bridge, where a left turn is made to ascend to the Trough of Bowland.

The Forest of Bowland is now bare moorland, wild and lonely, but penetrated by attractive valleys. The road climbs from one of these to the Trough of Bowland, a narrow two-mile-long pass reaching about 1000 feet, and linking Lancashire with West Yorkshire. Both the Forest and the Trough are popular with ramblers and cyclists, and the wise motorist parks his car and wanders for a while in one of the many wooded glades. From the highest point of the Trough there are fine views to the left of Morecambe Bay, with the Lakeland hills providing a dramatic backcloth.

Continue on the unclassified road to Abbeystead and the head waters of the river Wyre. The minor road forks right to continue to Lancaster 12 miles away, though an alternative is to take the left fork at Abbeystead, which descends to the A6 near Forton, where a right turn will bring you to Lancaster in 8 miles.

Appealing to Children
Lancaster Castle and the Lancaster Museum
White Scar Caves, Ingleton
Ingleborough Caves, near Clapham
Cliffe Castle Museum, Keighley
Bronte Museum, Haworth
Worth Valley Railway Museum, Haworth
Browsholme Hall, near Great Mitton

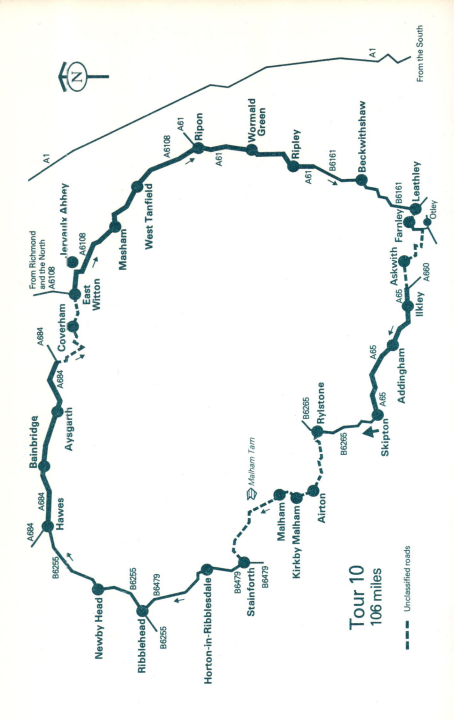

Tour 10
106 miles

‑ ‑ ‑ Unclassified roads

From the South

A1

From Richmond
and the North

Jervaulx Abbey

Ripon

Wormald Green

Ripley

Beckwithshaw

Leathley

Otley

Farnley

Askwith

West Tanfield

Masham

East Witton

Coverham

Ilkley

A660

Addingham

Bainbridge

Aysgarth

Rylstone

Malham Tarn

Skipton

Hawes

Malham

Kirkby Malham

Airton

Newby Head

Ribblehead

Horton-in-Ribblesdale

Stainforth

A1
A6108
A61
A61
A6108
A6108
A61
B6161
B6161
A65
A65
A65
A65
B6265
B6265
B6265
A684
A684
A684
A684
A684
B6255
B6255
B6479
B6479
B6479
B6255

10. The Yorkshire Dales: Wensleydale and Ribblesdale

This tour takes in much of Wensleydale as well as a large part of upper Ribblesdale. Starting from the old market town of Skipton, it includes many charming villages, the watershed of the Pennine moorlands, the beautifully-situated remains of Jervaulx Abbey and the remarkable limestone features of the Craven district. It is a tour which keeps away from towns in the main, but which provides impressive views of the desolate splendour of the Pennine range.

Skipton is a delightful town north of the Aire, with a broad, tree-lined main street. The great castle of the Cliffords, built in the 11th century and later, dominates this busy street. Approached through a gatehouse with rounded towers, the castle (open daily throughout the year) has a 50-ft.-long banqueting hall, a vast kitchen with roasting and baking hearths and a dungeon. Considering that it was under siege for three years during the Civil War, the remarkable feature of Skipton Castle is its state of preservation. The Town Hall, also in the High Street, houses the Skipton Craven Museum (open daily, except Tuesdays, throughout the year) with important exhibits of folk life, lead mining and Roman remains from the past history of the Craven district. A converted corn mill in Chapel Hill is the home of the George Leatt Industrial and Folk Museum (open on Sundays and Bank Holidays), with the mill restored to what it looked like in 1750, including a working water wheel. The Midland restaurant is recommended locally.

Leave Skipton by the B6265 for Rylestone, an attractive village in the limestone gap between the rivers Wharfe and the Aire. Turn left on to an unclassified road for Hetton, Airton and Kirkby Malham, where the road bends north and takes you into Malham.

Malham, an attractive village which gets very crowded during summer week-ends, has that kind of dramatic setting loved by film producers. Behind the village are sheer rock walls about 300 feet high, and to the east are the impressive cliffs of Gordale Scar, where waterfalls plunge down into a precipitous gorge. Malham Cove, about one mile north, is a much-photographed beauty spot, where the limestone cliffs form a curved back-cloth to a lovely wooded glen. Once the Aire flowed in a valley above the cliffs, but now it emerges as a stream at the foot of the cove. This awesome scenery was produced by earth movements during the Ice Age, and is a part of what is known as the North Craven Fault. Malham Tarn, north of the cove, is a quiet, upland lake in a shallow depression on a wide, green tableland. This is the setting

Skipton Castle: the gatehouse

for a part of Charles Kingsley's novel *The Water Babies,* which he
wrote at Tarn House on the north side of the lake.

*From the tarn take an unclassified road to the left, with many steep
and twisting hills, for Stainforth.*

Stainforth is a pleasant village with a 17th-century pack-horse
bridge over the Ribble.

*From Stainforth the route turns north along the B6479 to Horton-
in-Ribblesdale.*

Horton-in-Ribblesdale is a picturesque, moorland quarrying village
with a 12th- to 15th-century church. Quarries scar the fellsides
from Helwith Bridge to Horton, and a limestone works towers
behind the railway station. The twisted layers of rock to be seen
in the district are a magnet for geologists, and ramblers are
attracted to the village because of its easy accessibility to the fells.
Pen-y-Ghent (2373 ft.) rises to the north-east, and beneath the
mountain's slopes are several fine pot-holes, including Alum Pot,
Hunt Pot and Hull Pot.

*The B6479 follows the course of the upper Ribble valley, climbing
to Ribblehead where it reaches a junction with the B6255. Turn
right here to Newby Head, a farm on the watershed between the
Widdale Beck and the Gayle Beck, and then through the remote
Widdale to Hawes, 10 miles away.*

Hawes is a grey, old town standing 850 feet above sea level on the
river Ure, near the head of Wensleydale. It is the main marketing
centre for Swaledale sheep, as well as being a centre for
Wensleydale cheese. The wild surroundings of the town are more
impressive than the local buildings. South of Hawes, an
unclassified road runs through wild country across Fleet Moss
towards Langstrothdale. About 1 mile to the north is Hardraw
Force, a large waterfall cascading over a limestone ledge, and the
road leads over the Butter Tubs Pass.

*The A684 from Hawes follows the course of the river Ure through
the dale to Bainbridge.*

Bainbridge, now a pleasant village built round a wide green, was
once the centre of the great Forest of Wensleydale. For 700 years,
a hunting horn has been blown each evening from the village
green, a reminder of the times when the forest was so dense that
the sound of the horn was the only guide for lost travellers. The
river Bain flows down through the village from the Semerwater
Lake, a one-mile-long lake to the south, and on the east of the
river is Brough Hill topped by the remains of a Roman fort.
Follow a track from the village towards the Semerwater, and you
will be on the remains of a Roman road to Lancaster.

*Continue along the A684 to Aysgarth (described in Tour 8, page 48)
and on to Wensley, but shortly before the village turn right along an*

unclassified road for Coverham and East Witton.

Coverham is a hamlet in a delightful position at the foot of the upper part of Coverdale, with the remains of a 13th-century abbey built into an 18th-century house. East Witton is a village of old, greystone cottages built round an attractive tree-shaded green. The river Cover joins the Ure at this point.

At East Witton the A6108, turning right to Jervaulx Abbey.

Jervaulx Abbey is described in Tour 7, page 43).

The A6108 runs through the open, lower valley of the Ure to Masham (described in Tour 7, page 43) and Ripon.

Ripon (described in Tour 8, page 47) makes a good stopping place for refreshments on a route which has been mainly through open country and the Old Deanery restaurant is recommended locally.

From Ripon take the A61 to Ripley.

Ripley is also described in Tour 8, page 49.

1½ miles beyond, Ripley, fork right on to the B6161 for Killinghall and Beckwithshaw and on to Leathley.

Leathley, a pleasant hamlet on the Washburn near its junction with the Wharfe, has a church with an early-Norman tower which retains its original iron-bound door. 1½ miles away by an unclassified road, is Farnley Hall, the home of the Fawkes family whose ancestor was the notorious Guy Fawkes. This is an Elizabethan house with a splendid extension by John Carr of York. The artist J. M. W. Turner was a frequent visitor here, and the fine collection of paintings contains many of his works.

Follow the B6451 to Otley Bridge, turning right for Askwith and Ilkley.

Ilkley is described in Tour 7, page 41).

Leave Ilkley by the Skipton Road, the A65, and Skipton is reached in 9 miles.

Appealing to Children

Skipton Castle
Skipton Craven Museum and the George Leatt Folk Museum
Malham Cove
The Wakeman's Museum, Ripon
Ripley Castle